Cornwall Railw

on old picture p...........

Brian Lund and Paul Laming

1. The approach to **Bodmin** Great Western station, which opened in May 1887, on a postcard published by Frith of Reigate. It was later renamed Bodmin General. This station closed to passengers in January 1967, but has been resuscitated by the privately-run Bodmin-Wenford Railway, whose headquarters it now is. They run steam and diesel-hauled trains from the station.

Designed and published by
Reflections of a Bygone Age,
Keyworth, Nottingham, 2007

Printed by Phase, Underwood,
Nottinghamshire

£3.95

Introduction

The romance of railway travel and its resulting nostalgia is nowhere more evident than in memories of the Golden Age of railways in Cornwall, where services were dominated by the Great Western company - though the London & South Western had the run of the north of the county. Both these major operations took over smaller companies, such as the Bodmin & Wadebridge or the West Cornwall, which had originally built the Cornish lines. This book aims to provide a flavour of the early 20th century, when both Britain's railways and picture postcards had their 'Golden Age'. A hundred years ago, it was possible to travel round Cornwall easily by train, with most villages served by passenger traffic. Now only a basic main line network survives, though four branch lines still run to Looe, Newquay, Falmouth and St Ives.

The choice of illustrations in this book has been governed entirely by what picture postcards are available. Between 1902 and 1918, postcards, which cost half the letter rate to post, were used as the normal form of communication for greetings and brief news or information messages. *"I will arrive tomorrow on the 2.30 train"*, was a typical instruction, with the sender totally confident that the card would be delivered the following day. A host of national and local firms published cards, but the choice of views was entirely at the whim or commercial strategem of the publisher. Thus it is easy to find postcard views of Penzance, where national firms like Valentine of Dundee found it profitable to produce cards to a potentially large buying public, while Chacewater has proved amazingly elusive. It was left to small local publishers - who often remained anonymous - to publish views of the village railway station, probably in very small quantities. One bonus, however, is that WH Smith, who had a bookstall on all the important stations in England, usually published at least one postcard view of all those stations.

It is not surprising that there was a ready sale for postcards of railway stations. Along with the church, pub and post office, the station was the hub of a village community, the place where goods left and arrived, and villagers set off on a visit to the nearest town or a more adventurous destination.

We hope you will enjoy this nostalgic selection of railway postcards.

Brian Lund
June 2007

Front cover: a train at Praze station on the branch line from Helston to Gwinear Road. It saw its last passenger train on 23rd November 1962. The postcard was published c.1908, when the branch had nine trains each way daily, and two on Sundays.

Back cover (top): a superb photographic image of the railway station at Perranporth on a postcard published by S Harvey Mitchell. It was posted from Perranporth to Norwich in May 1905 with the message including the question *"Do you know this place?"*
Back cover (bottom): the distinctive architecture of Penzance railway station on a postcard published by J Welch of Portsmouth, posted at Penzance in November 1908.

Acknowledgments: thanks to Roger Lacy, who provided some caption notes, and illustrations 56 and 58.

2. Postcard published by F Moore of the interior of **Bodmin**'s London & South-Western railway station, opened in November 1895. Renamed Bodmin North in September 1949, it closed to passengers in January 1967.

3. Bodmin Road (now Bodmin Parkway) on the Great Western Railway's main line, where passengers could change for Bodmin, Wadebridge and Padstow, was opened in June 1889. The branch line to Bodmin closed in 1967, but is now used by the preserved Bodmin-Wenford Railway. The publisher of this postcard is unknown, a not unusual feature of Edwardian vintage postcards - many were produced anonymously.

S.11701   APPROACH TO L. & S.W. RLY. STATION, BUDE.

4. The London & South Western railway station at **Bude** on a card published by WH Smith in their 'Kingsway' series. Bude, which was used from 1898-1967, was at the end of a branch off the Okehampton - Wadebridge line at Halwill Junction. Eight trains a day left Bude in 1910, with just one on Sundays. That departed at 6.52 am, reaching Okehampton at 8.04 am.

5. Burngullow was on the Great Western main line between St. Austell and Grampound Road. The branch on the right is still open for china clay traffic to Parkandillack. There were two stations on this site, the second closing to passengers in September 1931. This postcard was published by JB Sherlock.

6. Frith c.1907 postcard of **Calstock** station on what a century ago was the Plymouth, Devonport & South-Western Junction Railway between Bere Alstock and Callington. The branch now terminates at Gunnislake, though Calstock station is still open to passengers as a 'request' stop, goods traffic having ceased in February 1966. In 1910, six trains ran in each direction daily.

S 10771   CALLINGTON STATION, P.D. & S.W. JUN. RLY

7. Callington, at the end of this line from Bere Alston, portrayed on another WH Smith 'Kingsway' series card. The firm published postcards of every station where they had a bookstall. This station was actually located at Kelly Bray, from where buses took passengers to Callington. The station closed in November 1966.

8. Callington on a Frith-published postcard from about 1906, when the town had a population of 1,700.

RAILWAY STATION, CAMBORNE

S 6990

9. Camborne on the main Great Western line to Penzance. It was opened by the West Cornwall Railway in February 1852, and the GWR took complete control in January 1866. WH Smith published the postcard.

10. The interior of **Camborne** station on a postcard from the prolific Illogan firm of Bragg.

11. Carbis Bay is still open on the GWR branch from St. Erth to St. Ives. The station served a hamlet, delivering mostly holidaying passengers. Carbis Bay is now a growing suburb of St. Ives.

L. & S. W. Railway Station, Del

12. Delabole, on the London & South Western Railway line between Okehampton and Wadebridge via Halwill Junction, opened in October 1893 and closed in October 1966. It was a terminus until June 1895, when the line to Wadebridge opened. Delabole boasted quarries producing *"the finest slate in*

e, R. S. O. Cornwall.

T. Harris's Series, Quethiock, Liskeard.

the kingdom", according to a 1904 gazetteer. This postcard was published by T Harris, Quethiock, Liskeard.

13. Falmouth, at the end of the Great Western branch from Truro, is still open, but this original station was closed by British Railways in 1970 and replaced by a new single-platform facility (at first named 'The Dell' and now 'Falmouth Town') nearer the town.

14. A postcard of **Fowey** station posted in October 1905. The station for the seaside port and resort (population in 1904, 2,258) enabled passengers to take trains for either St Blazey (until July 1929) or Par (until January 1965, when Fowey closed for passenger trains). Freight still operates on part of the branch, from Lostwithiel to Carne Point. It was also carried from St Blazey until August 1968, when that line was converted into a private road for lorries taking china clay traffic.

15. Goonbell Halt opened in August 1905 on the Newquay-Chacewater line, which had three intermediate stations and seven halts from July 1931, with Perranporth Beach Halt the last to be opened. Local trains called at all the stations and halts. The village of Goonbell is a mile south-east of St. Agnes. The halt closed in February 1963.

16. Grampound Road station, which had its own post office, opened in May 1859, between Burngullow and Truro on the Great Western main line. The village it served, famous for being a 'rotten borough' sending two members to parliament until it was disenfranchised, lay two miles south-east and had a population of under 500 in Edwardian days. The station closed in October 1964.

17. A postcard of **Grampound Road** posted to a corporal in the 21st battalion the London Regiment at Howls Green Camp, Sittingbourne, in 1908. *"Hope you will have a jolly time at Sittingbourne. Do you recognise this place? We are having some rotten weather"*.

18. Chapman of Dawlish published this card of **Gunnislake** on the Plymouth, Devonport & South-Western Junction Railway's line from Bere Alston to Callington. Goods traffic ceased in February 1966, but passenger trains still use what is actually a new station terminus, opened in June 1994, on the opposite side of the A390 road.

19. Helston on a postcard published by the London firm of Stengel in 1904. The station, opened in May 1887 at the end of a branch from Gwinear Road on the Great Western main line, closed to passengers in November 1962 and to goods in October 1964.

20. Another postcard of **Helston** station interior, published about 1920 by an unidentified firm.

Launceston, St. Stephens.

21. Launceston's two stations were adjacent, serving both the GWR and LSWR. The former closed to passengers in June 1952, the latter in October 1966. The Great Western opened in July 1865, the London & South Western in July 1886, both as termini. This changed in July 1892 when the LSWR line was extended to Tresmeer. From 1952-1966, British Rail trains on the former GWR line used the LSWR station.

22. Lelant on a 1923 card. This station is still open on the branch line to St. Ives.

23. Liskeard on the Great Western main line is pictured on a postcard published by Francis Frith of Reigate, one of the biggest producers of topographical postcards in the early 20th century.

24. Liskeard station about 1904 on a postcard published by Stengel. This station is now the first (or last!) place to see semaphore signals on the Penzance-Paddington line.

25. Looe station, at the end of a branch line from Liskeard, is still open. The passenger service to Looe from Moorswater Junction began in September 1879. The station platform at Looe is now shorter than seen on this postcard, which was published c.1910 by the photographer E Pouteau, a prolific producer of railway postcards.

26. Looe on a postcard published by Hartmann and posted in 1917. Considerable promotion has been aimed at the Looe branch in recent years, with the winter service now nine trains each way Monday to Saturday.

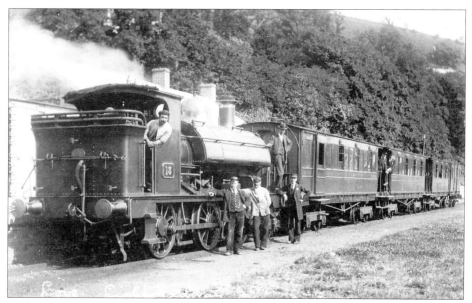

27. A scene at **Looe** on a card published by E Pouteau of London. The train engineers, station staff and pasengers have all been co-opted to pose for the photographer.

28. Nanstallon Halt between Wadebridge and Bodmin on the LSWR line. Opened in July 1906, it closed in January 1967.

29. Marazion, the last station before Penzance on the Great Western main line, closed to passenger trains in October 1964, and completely in December 1965. When it first opened in March 1852, it was known as Marazion Road.

Station - Newquay.

30. Newquay. A Stengel-published postcard postally used in September 1907. Goods traffic to Newquay ceased in September 1964, but the station is still open as the terminus of a branch line from Par. This picture was taken after construction of the island platform in the autumn of 1904. Since 1987, all the structures seen here have been demolished, and only one platform is in use. The station is unstaffed apart from the peak summer season.

31. Station staff at **Chacewater** on a card published by SJ Govier of Chacewater and St. Agnes. The station, on the Truro to Penzance section of the Great Western main line, closed to both passenger and goods traffic in October 1964.

32. Otterham, opened in August 1893, was on the Halwill Junction-Wadebridge section of the LSWR. It closed to goods traffic in September 1964 and to passengers in October 1966.

33. Padstow on a card published by Valentine of Dundee. It was the end of the road for the LSWR branch from Wadebridge, now converted to a cycleway called 'The Camel Trail'. In 1910 it was possible to take a seven-hour train ride to the seaside resort from London Waterloo via Exeter. The land on the right is now a car park for a lobster hatchery and cycle hire premises.

34. Padstow's station, opened in March 1899, closed in January 1967. In the early 19th century, it hosted eleven passenger trains each way daily, but none on Sundays. Part of the station building is now used by Padstow Town Council.

35. Par, still open on the Great Western main line, is the junction for Newquay. Goods traffic ceased in June 1964. This card was published by Kathleen Rundell of Par.

36. A flooded **Par** station c. 1907. The Newquay platform is on the right
direction. There are still four trains daily from Monday to Saturday, with

10, five passenger trains went to Newquay daily, and four in the reverse
n summer, including trains from Paddington and the north of England.

37. Par, seen on a postcard published c.1920 by S Daley-Smith, St. Blazey.

38. Penryn is still open on the Great Western's Truro-Falmouth branch, but has just one platform on what is now a single line.

39. Penryn on a c.1908 postcard published by Valentine.

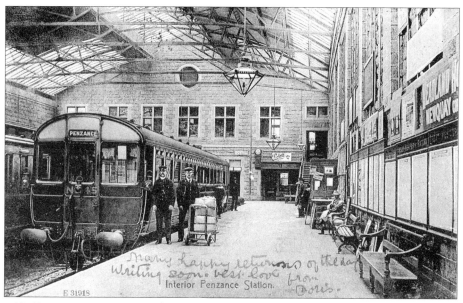

40. Penzance. A rail motor stands in the station on this card published by Stengel and postally used in December 1906. The station is the terminus of the Great Western Railway's main line from London Paddington, and is adjacent to both the bus station and the Tourist Information office.

41. Perranporth on a Bragg-published postcard. This station was opened in July 1903 as a terminus on the GWR line from Chacewater. It became a through station when the line was extended to Newquay in January 1905. It closed in February 1963. The coastal village of Perranporth was noted for pilchard fishing and tin mining in the 19th century, but both these had virtually ceased by the time the railway was built.

42. Perranwell on the Truro - Falmouth line is still open. This c.1920 postcard was published by JB Sherlock.

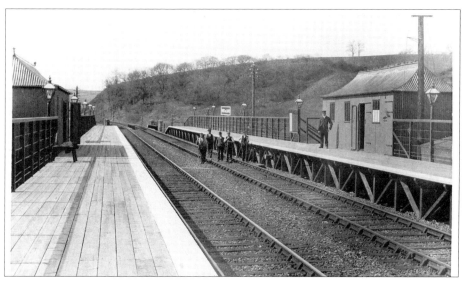

43. Probus & Ladock GWR platform, opened in February 1908, was on the line between Truro and Grampound Road, but it closed in December 1957.

Motor Train
Saltash Station

44. Saltash was 'the gateway to Cornwall' on the Great Western's main line. This card, showing a rail motor in the station, was published by CA Pratt of Saltash in the 'Pharmacy' series, posted at Devonport in September 1906. The coming of the railway to Saltash revived a declining town, increasing its prosperity. Once the Tamar road bridge opened in 1961, though, rail commuter traffic was drastically reduced. Today, nine trains in each direction stop at Saltash on weekdays.

Cornishmen leaving Redruth R. Station
for the African Goldfields. 6

45. Cornishmen leaving **Redruth** for the African goldfields. The station was opened in March 1852 by the West Cornwall Railway. Card published by Martin of Redruth.

46. Saltash on a card posted to Fratton in June 1918. *"Thought you would like a view of Saltash"*. This is a common postcard view of Saltash station, with Brunel's Albert Bridge in the background.

47. St. Agnes GWR station on the Chacewater - Newquay line opened in July 1903 and closed in February 1963. In 1937, the station was rebuilt with an island platform, signal box and a crossing point facility for two trains to pass each other. The seaport town had a population of 4,291 in 1910; its harbour fell into disuse during World war One.

48. St. Agnes on a postcard published by Solway.

49. A works outing at **St. Austell** station. Local photographers often published events and celebrations as picture postcards.

50. St. Austell GWR station on a postcard published by Frith in 1912. The bus station is now on the left of the picture, with a car park on the right. The station has new buildings on the downside (left), and the water column has gone, but the footbridge remains.

51. St. Blazey was the intermediate station on the four-and-a-half mile Par to Fowey branch line. This was the first station opened by the Cornwall Minerals Railway in June 1874. It was on the direct line from Fowey to Newquay, with a connecting line to the GWR main line at Par opening five years later. It closed to passengers in July 1929 and to goods traffic in June 1964. This postcard was published by Frith of Reigate, and posted at Padstow in October 1904.

52. St. Erth, a Great Western main line station and junction for St. Ives, on a c.1905 postcard. This was opened by the West Cornwall Railway in March 1852, and was known as St. Ives Road until the opening of the St. Ives branch in June 1877.

53. St. Ives on a card published by Valentine of Dundee about 1905, when 13 trains ran to and from St. Erth daily, four on Sundays. Today, the line still has a very frequent service.

54. Workmen at **Shepherds** station c. 1907. A common feature of postcards featuring railway stations was the way that station and railway staff were often seen posing for the photographer.

S 2574   GREAT WESTERN RAILWAY STATION, TRURO.

55. Truro. Card published c.1912 (though the picture dates from c.1905, as the cathedral has only one spire) by WH Smith in their 'Kingsway' series.

56. A group of well-dressed Edwardian travellers waits at **Goonhaven Halt** on the Chacewater-Newquay line, which opened in August 1905 and closed in February 1963. Since closure, the village of Goonhaven has seen considerable growth, as have others on this line. An anonymously-published postcard.